THE
"I HATE KATHIE LEE GIFFORD"
BOOK

THE
"I HATE KATHIE LEE GIFFORD"
BOOK

Gary Blake
and Robert W. Bly

KENSINGTON BOOKS
http://www.kensingtonbooks.com

KENSINGTON BOOKS are published by

Kensington Publishing Corp.
850 Third Avenue
New York, NY 10022

ISBN 1-57566-144-6

First Printing: February, 1997
10 9 8 7 6 5 4 3 2 1

Printed in the United States of America

"You can call me he, you can call me she,
You can call me Regis and Kathie Lee."

—RUPAUL, 6′6″ transvestite model
spokesperson for Mack cosmetics

"She's just too damn perky."

—ROCKY ALLEN, <u>The Rocky Allen Showgram,</u>
WPLJ 95.5 FM, New York

"She is so fine,
she can turn bread into wine."

—Scott and Todd on <u>The Morning Show</u>
on WPLJ-FM 95.5 FM, New York:

"Being a celebrity basically stinks."

—Kathy Lee Gifford

"I always feel I'm letting somebody down, no matter what I do."

—Kathy Lee Gifford

ACKNOWLEDGMENTS

This book is no one's fault but ours.

DEDICATION

To every American who is not a celebrity.

WARRANTY

The authors warrant that everyone associated with this book has been paid more than the minimum wage, with the possible exception of the authors themselves. We also warrant that, if any labor violations have occurred in relation to the production of this book, Kathie Lee Gifford knew nothing about them. She takes no responsibility whatsoever. In fact, we believe she doesn't have a clue.

Introduction

She's gorgeous.

She's perky.

She's married to a football hero.

She's a TV star.

She's rich and famous.

She has two adorable children, three cute dogs,
and a big house in Connecticut.

Couldn't you just puke?

Although at times it seems as if everyone loves Kathie
Lee Gifford, maybe you—like us—think she is just a
wee bit too perfect and needs to be taken down a peg
or two. As Tim Connor, coauthor of *Is Martha Stewart
Living?*, points out, authoritarian figures need to be
poked fun at, "so they don't take themselves too seri-

ously." That's what we aim to do, in an entertaining fashion, in THE "I HATE KATHIE LEE GIFFORD" BOOK.

Look behind the facade and you see the sham that is her life.

- Her husband is an ex-football player who holds the record for most forward passes . . . caught on the head.

- She says she is a champion of the poor and down-trodden, yet spends more on Christmas ornaments than most American families spend on food in a year.

- She is so wholesome she makes Julie Andrews gag. Even Mother Theresa won't return her calls.

- She has a vocabulary of approximately 187 words (if you count "adorable," "Cody," "Regis," and "Frank").

- She has never eaten a hot pastrami sandwich in her life.

- She buys her Christmas tree the week after Labor Day . . . and amazingly, it seems to stay fresh well past New Year's.

Like us, you may be asking yourself: Who is this lady? Our investigative report uncovers the real Kathie Lee (the woman behind the lip gloss) by taking a no-holds-barred look at everything from her politics to her sex life, from her children to her TV career, from her record albums to her endorsements.

We'll see her arguing with Frank ("Frank, put your teeth in when you talk to me!"), buying him gifts (a gold-plated walker), writing in her diary ("Once again I have impure thoughts about Pauli Shore . . ."), cursing ("Oy vey!"), and her fears for her son (rumor has it he is dis-interested in football, talks back to Frank, and is an ag-nostic.)

We have written this book for every American who is not perfect—and who has a sneaking suspicion that Kathie Lee, America's favorite Stepford Wife, isn't either.

This book proves that she and her family are real. She gets yeast infections. Frank uses Fixodent. Cody leaves his coat on the floor. Regis, the household dog, sometimes misses the newspaper when he poops. She hasn't memorized the Bible . . . yet. And she gets ticked off every time Frank roams around the house whistling, "When I'm 64."

A Kathie Lee Chronology

1953, August 16—

Kathie Lee Epstein born in Paris. Star of Bethlehem seen in the night sky. Meanwhile, in the United States, Frank Gifford celebrates his 23rd birthday with no thoughts of "robbing the cradle."

1957—

Family returns to U.S., disliking French food. Lives in Bowie, Maryland, and consumes large quantities of hard-shell crabs.

1965—

Kathie Lee takes first walk with God. He falls asleep on park bench. During walk, God asks, "Is Epstein your real name?"

1971—

Kathie Lee voted Maryland's Junior Miss, narrowly defeating a young Marie Osmond. Becomes Anita Bryant's live-in personal assistant. Commodities traders suffer large losses in orange juice futures.

1972—

Anita Bryant arranges for Kathie Lee Gifford to attend Oral Roberts University.

1975—

Kathie Lee moves to California. No earthquakes registered that year.

1976—

Kathie Lee's first book, *The Quiet Riot,* is published. Over 10 copies sold.

Kathie Lee marries Paul Johnson. Is rumored to have said at wedding, "I always wanted a Johnson."

1977-1978—

Kathie Lee Gifford is "la-la" lady on *$100,000 Name That Tune.* Repairs of television sound systems increase 15 percent for the year.

1978—

Kathie Lee receives patent on non-smear lip gloss. Later awarded Nobel Prize in chemistry for the invention.

1979—

Kathie Lee becomes a *Hee-Haw* Honey—a milestone in American television.

1983—

Kathie Lee Gifford becomes spokesperson for Carnival Cruise Lines. Air travel increases 15 percent for the year.

1985—

Kathie Lee joins Regis Philbin on ABC's *Morning Show*. The authors of this book decide to sleep in.

1986, October 18—

Marries Frank Gifford in Bridgehampton, N.Y. Minister bills for services at AARP discount rate.

1989—

Morning Show goes into national syndication as *Live with Regis and Kathie Lee*. Civilization as we know it ends.

1990—

Cody is born.

Kathie Lee signs on to promote Home Furnishing Council—selling couches to couch potatoes.

1992—

Publishes *I Can't Believe I Said That!* No one else can, either.

1993—

Initiates feud with producer Michael Gelman, who briefly considers enrolling in rabbinical school.

1994—

Kathie Lee Gifford featured on *McCall's* cover twice. We cancel our subscription.

1995—

Kathie Lee signs up to promote Wal★Mart. We start shopping at Kmart.

Howard Stern initiates feud with Kathie Lee Gifford.

Kathie Lee publishes *Listen to My Heart: Lessons in Love, Laughter, and Lunacy.* We decide to wait for the movie.

Kathie Lee Gifford announces she will no longer participate in the Miss America pageant. People still watch anyway.

Sings the national anthem at the Super Bowl. Frank Gifford rushes onto the field and, mistaking her for the quarterback of the opposing team, sacks her.

Meets President and Mrs. Clinton. Hillary asks her, "How come you never mention your daughter?"

Kathie Lee's holiday special airs on TV. One critic comments, "She's berserk. She's crazed. She's out of control."

1996—

Rumor that Kathie Lee Gifford will replace Julie Andrews in *Victor/Victoria*.

On May 1, Kathie Lee answers a report that some of the clothes in her Wal★Mart clothing line were made by underpaid child labor in Honduras. She berates the labor group that visited the sweatshop in Honduras and broke the story.

On May 23, *The New York Daily News* uncovers a New York City sweatshop that also makes blouses for Kathie Lee's Wal-Mart clothing line. Frank Gifford offers to pay the wages of everyone in the factory. "I have the money," he tells a reporter, "I just need to know who the hell they are." He hopes they can break $100.

Late breaking story—

Kathie Lee discovers that exploitation in the American work force is quite common. Offers to pay the national debt and to take downsized sweatshop personnel with her on a Carnival cruise where she will offer outplacement seminars, light refreshments, and entertainment by the Christy Minstrel trio.

27 People We'd
on a Desert

1. Kathie Lee Gifford

2. Ann Landers

3. Phyllis Schlafly

4. Raffi

5. Ross Perot

6. The Ayatollah Khomeini

7. O.J. Simpson

Rather Not be Stuck Island With

8. Miss Manners

9. Morton Downey, Jr.

10. Sally Jesse Raphael

11—12. The Menendez brothers

13. Dr. Kevorkian

14. The Reverend Al Sharpton

15—27. Any of the O.J. jurors

Kathie Lee's 12 Favorite Films of All Time

1. *The Picture of Dorian Gray*

2. *It's a Wonderful Life*

3. *Love Story*

4. *Mary Poppins*

5. *The Sound of Music*

6. *Dumb and Dumber*

7. *Bambi*

8. *Beauty and the Beast*

9. *It's a Wonderful Life*

10. *It's a Wonderful Life*

11. *Sounder*

12. *It's a Wonderful Life*

Christmas and Birthday Gifts Kathie Lee Always Returns or Exchanges

1.

Bagel cutter

2.

The Club

3.

Subscription to *The Village Voice*

4.

Encyclopedia Britannica

5.

Ron Popeil's Pocket Fisherman

Kathie Lee's List of Ten Great Women in the 20th Century

1. Estee Lauder
2. Priscilla Presley
3. Mary Kay
4. Mother Theresa
5. Anita Bryant
6. Sandy Duncan
7. Tori Spelling
8. Donna Karan
9. Sally Struthers
10. Golda Meir

The Kathie Lee's Day Planner Week of August 15

Monday—

Fix Cody's beeper

Give Frank enema

Call Howard Stern

Accept award from *TV Guide*

Tuesday—

Learn words to national anthem

Watch *Third Rock from the Sun*—have Cody explain jokes to me

Bring Cody and Cassidy to Ben and Jerry's

Wednesday—

Rent truck

Bring clothes to dry cleaner

Buy lip gloss

Be perky!

Put $25 in business account

Make out weekly payroll to sweatshop workers

Thursday—

Spend a few minutes this morning preparing for Stephen Hawking interview

Spend weekend preparing for Marlo Thomas interview

Friday—

Buy lox at deli

Get manicure

Whiten teeth

Saturday—

Learn the Macarena

Go to beauty parlor

Sunday—

Build in some "down time" to decompress

Form the Kathie Lee Gifford Holding Company

Take over Cap Cities ABC

The Six Best Kathie Lee Gifford Jokes

1.

What do Kathie Lee and Barbie have in common?

They both sell out during the holidays.

2.

Why did Kathie Lee marry Frank Gifford?

Bob Hope was already in a relationship.

3.

Does Frank ever get tired of keeping up with Kathie Lee?

At his age, Frank gets tired of everything.

We've Ever Heard

4.

Kathie Lee thinks "downsizing" is when you go from size 8 to size 6.

5.

Kathie Lee thinks "out-sourcing" is when you give the cook the night off.

6.

Why did Kathie Lee cross the road?

To avoid making eye contact with the Honduran sweatshop worker walking toward her.

The Kathie Lee Gifford Glossary

What she says . . .

"Wuggies"

"I'll pray for you"

"I've always been very approval-oriented"

"I'm so embarrassed by the blessings I have. Enough is enough."

"I hate my upper thighs with a passion."

"I want to spend more time with my family."

# of Euphemisms

What she means . . .

"Bulging thighs"

"Cross me again and you're history!"

"Cross me again and you're history!"

"I wonder where Marla Trump shops for emeralds?"

"I hate my upper thighs with a passion."

"I'm planning a leveraged buy-out of Carnival Cruise lines this weekend."

The Unexpurgated Kathie Lee Gifford Diaries

CONTENTS PERSONAL AND CONFIDENTIAL. PENALTY FOR VIOLATION: You'll be forced to watch 40 consecutive episodes of my show

January 10—

Secret lunch meeting with Martha Stewart to discuss "Connecticut Cuisine" book project. When I arrived at her home, Martha was just finishing building a nuclear power plant out of cranberries.

We divided the chapters between us. I have a month to write mine, including Bridgeport Brisket, Norton Nachos, Fairfield Falafels, Westport Waffles, and Stamford Steamers.

REMINDER! Pack peanut butter paté snack for Cody's lunch box.

January 19—

Once again had impure thoughts about Pee Wee Herman . . .

January 27—

Frank was complaining about his arthritis again. Felt like throwing the Motrin at him. He is always complaining. Misplaced his Social Security check the other day and blamed the nanny. His biggest worry: soon he'll be forced to take money out of his Keogh account. Honestly, the things he frets about! It's always, "Kathie Lee, where are my football cuff links?" "Kathie Lee, what time is *The Simpsons* on?" "Kathie Lee, my chest pains are getting worse; call an ambulance." What a kvetch!

February 15—

Started recording the new show tunes album. Sounded in good form. May title the record, *I Got Plenty O Nothin'* . . .

February 28—

Must remember to take the Christmas tree out front to be hauled away. Attended 20th college reunion. Former classmate told fascinating story about how Oral Roberts got his name . . .

March 17—

Broke another nail. Is the Lord testing me in some way?

March 18—

This Wal★Mart thing is getting on my nerves. They actually expect me to *wear* the crap I make! They can't pay me enough to do *that!*

Reminder: Ask Frank if there's a way to donate our frequent flyer miles to underprivileged children who fly only coach.

March 30—

Showed our Manhattan co-op to someone we're hoping the co-op board will approve. His name is Al Sharpton. Apparently, he is a man of the cloth—and from the look of him, of the buffet as well.

April 4—

Passover with Gelman again. Bo-ring! Took me till morning to find the Afakomen . . . and then Gelman only paid me five dollars. Once again, his pal "Elijah" didn't show. Sang "Dayenu" and only received scale . . .

April 15—

Ironically, received our tax refund today. Went out and bought three Hawaiian islands.

April 16—

My birthday! Frank bought me Vancouver!

April 19—

McCall's wants me to be on the cover of their July issue. Also, they want me to write an article about anything I want, except Anita Bryant. On another topic: Why do I find Mario Perillo so sexy? Also: Why do they call him "Mr. Italy" when his last name, obviously, is Perillo? I'm going to ask our viewers to write me . . .

Reminder: Must remember to ask Reege who "C.D. ROM" is? Keep hearing his name. Can we book him for a segment next week? If he's Jewish, won't have any trouble convincing Gelman.

April 28—

Regis can be so mean. Today, he called me "voluptuous" on TV. I'm going to look it up in that book that has all the words in it to see what it means. He's always putting me down because he thinks he's so intelligent and I'm so dumb. Why? I don't make fun of his singing, which absolutely sucks.

Reminder: Unless they come up with the mortgage payment, foreclose on the Trumps' house. No excuses.

Note: Find out about this new support hose I keep hearing about—Internet. Want my legs to look their best!

Kathie Lee's 10 Favorite Words...

1. adorable
2. perfect
3. love
4. sharing
5. Cody
6. God
7. Bible
8. Frank
9. me
10. lip gloss

...and 10 Words and Expressions You'll Rarely Hear Kathie Lee Utter

1. Oy vey!

2. *Gott Sei Dunk!*

3. Right On!

4. synchronicity

5. yeast infection

6. I could care less.

7. You piss me off!

8. I've heard good things about the new Philip Roth book.

9. I insist Cody get bar mitzvahed!

10. I see your point.

Kathie Lee Gifford Stupid Comment #3

To a movie star about to be featured in a film version of *Middlemarch*, by George Eliot:

"I love all of his books!"

As every college freshman knows, George Eliot was the pen name of Mary Ann Evans. It beats the hell out of us why people think you're a phony! Perhaps you just hate to be left out of a good discussion, regardless of how little you can add to it?

Our Theory on Why Kathie Lee and Regis Work So Well Together

Rarely do you find two people with precisely the same lack of intellectual development. Both of them are so blatantly ignorant of the world around them that when they converse, they make each other, by comparison, seem smart.

Watching them try to top each other, knowing neither will ever rise to either wit or wisdom, is one of the comforting things about the show. You'll never be in danger of having to ponder a serious subject for more than three minutes.

Example: On April 10, 1996, Regis and Kathie spent *seven* minutes discussing the use of coyote urine as a way of keeping deer off your property. On *Live with Regis and Kathie Lee,* gun control, abortion, terrorism, Whitewater, Bosnia, and the Middle East take a back seat to deer pee-pee.

From the "Believe it or Not" Files

Nielson Families Go Insane—

When Cody Newton Gifford, Kathie Lee's son, appeared on *Live with Regis and Kathie Lee*, four out of every ten TV viewers in New York City tuned in—the syndicated program's highest NYC share ever.

The American Public Must Know Something We Don't . . .

According to The New York Daily News, Kathie Lee's "Home for Christmas" special was the highest-rated Christmas special of 1995. Good grief, Charlie Brown!

Please take our names off the mailing list...

For a 15-issue subscription to the *Live with Regis & Kathie Lee* newsletter, send $20 (payable to "Live Newsletter") to:

> Subscription Coupon,
> PO Box 2010,
> Floral Park, New York 11002.

Recent articles include retail outlets where you can buy Kathie Lee's fashions and Martha Stewart's recipe for stuffed mushrooms.

10 Things Kathie Lee Would Prefer You Not Know About Her

1. Attracted to Nitro from American Gladiators

2. Attracted to Ice from American Gladiators

3. A huge *Doogie Howser* fan

4. When no one's looking, drinks Dom Perignon right out of the bottle

5. Bad foot odor problem

6. Frank reminds her of "Grandpa Lee" when walking around the house nude

7. Honorary member of the Hair Club for Men

8. Nods off in church during the sermon

9. Hates small talk

10. Owns Regis Philbin voodoo doll

More From the BELIEVE IT OR NOT Files

When *TV Guide* asked readers to call in and vote for the "Most Beautiful Woman on TV," Kathie Lee Gifford won, with 17,796.

Even more amazing was that the first runner-up—former "Charlie's Angel" Jaclyn Smith—received only 3,603 votes . . . less than one-fifth the number received by Kathie Lee!

What these statistics *don't* tell you is that Kathie Lee actively campaigned to win this contest, asking her viewers repeatedly to vote for her the week of the contest.

At one point, she appeared with pom poms and led a "Vote for Me!" cheer.

She also had her son Cody on air, dialing *TV Guide's* 900 number on camera.

Kathie Lee defends her self-promotion campaign to win the *TV Guide* "Most Beautiful Woman on TV" contest, noting: "It was meant as total sarcasm and self-mockery."

Second String: Women We Think Should Get a Tryout to Replace Kathie Lee Gifford if She Quits as Regis Philbin's Co-Host

Paula Barbieri

Marcia Clark

Betty Ford

Salt 'n Pepa

Pepa (by herself)

Mother Theresa

Richard Simmons

Anna Nicole Smith

Kathy Ireland

The tall brunette model from the *Victoria's Secret* catalogs

Geraldine Ferraro

Any of the female members of the Partridge Family

Shirley MacLaine's next incarnation

Sally Field

Queen Elizabeth

Vicki, the *Time-Life* operator

The most recent winner of the Publisher's Clearinghouse $10 million sweepstakes

Carnie

Taking Care of Business

TO: My "So Called" Agent
FROM: Kathie Lee
RE: Amending my contract with ABC

Before long it will be contract time again and I just wanted to go over a few points with you about new provisions based on the ratings the show has achieved. Don't get me wrong. I'm just a simple, sweet person who asks nothing more than to contribute to charity, be a good wife to Frank, and keep Cody happy. But the time has come for the show to recognize my contribution. Therefore, I'd like you to request the following from the network:

1. I'd like a larger dressing room. The one I have now is getting cramped. Who would have thought an indoor pool would take up so much room? The Nautilus equipment was a help, but I think I need more space to exercise. I hear basketball really takes the pounds off. If they could build a basketball court near my dressing table I could get in a few minutes of foul shooting before the show airs . . . I have started to macramé the fabric that hangs from the basketball hoops, and I've asked Martha Stewart to suggest some designer colors for the basketballs . . .

2. *Cody's office needs new wall-to-wall carpeting.* Ever since his canary vomited on the powder blue carpet, the whole look has been thrown off. Now my son, as you know, is not a complainer, but I am his mother and I do feel he should have the best possible office, even though he is reluctant to appear on the show again. Who knows when the Codes will change his sweet little mind? Saw some thick woolen carpet that we can get on sale for $185 a square yard. No need to pay full price. Look at the bargain I got on his Jacuzzi!

3. *The limo.* Look, I'm just a down-home kinda gal, but I have been asking for more than a month to get the air conditioning fixed in my limo. Can someone look into this please? It takes, sometimes, more than 20 seconds for the cool air to reach me. This could be because stretch limos are so long, or it could be faulty wiring. In any case, please do look into it. Also: the windows. Is it just me, or has anyone else noticed something funny about the windows? They go up. They go down. But I can't get them to go sideways. An oversight? I think not. I see Regis's hand in this! One other thing. I opened the sunroof on the limo and guess what? You got it: NO SUN!!! I don't want excuses. Fix it and fix it fast!!!!

4. Again, about the limo: Explain once again why it's impractical to have a cable dish for the limo? The reception sucks! Also, remember when Cody took his friends to miniature golf and they wanted to have pizza in the limo? I couldn't find a button that sets up a dining room table. Is he supposed to eat it on his lap?? Call the limo's manufacturer and ask if this model has been recalled, OK?

5. The limo driver.   A sweet man, no doubt. But this man has the gall to keep showing me pictures of his kids! I mean, what kind of ego does it take to assume that a perfect stranger would be interested in details about his children? Some people! Honestly!

Bald-faced Kathie Lee Gifford Lie #22: "I'm Jewish"

Reason said: To defend herself when accused of making anti-Semitic remarks about her producer, Michael Gelman.

The reality: Her father is half-Jewish. Kathie Lee was raised as a Christian. And she attends church regularly today.

Kathie Lee's Four Biggest Complaints About Being 1/4 Jewish:

1. At Hanukkah, she is only allowed to light two candles.

2. At Passover, she gets to read only one of the four questions.

3. On Yom Kippur, she can only fast for six hours.

4. She only has to obey 2 1/2 of the ten commandments.

Six Ways in Which Frank Gifford is Different From a Piece of Furniture

1. Furniture brightens a room.

2. Furniture has a function in life.

3. Furniture is mobile.

4. Furniture just doesn't lie there—it supports you.

5. Furniture is a welcome addition to any household.

6. Most furniture is no longer made from wood.

Kathie Lee's Recipe for Thanksgiving Turkey Dinner with All the Fixin's

1. Tell the cook to make dinner.

2. Eat dinner.

3. Tell the maid to clear the table and wash the dishes.

4. Watch Frank loosen his belt and fall asleep on the couch.

Kathie Lee Stupid and Offensive Comment #9

(To her 5-year-old son, Cody):

"I won't talk about you on the show if it's not okay with you. But then Mommy's going to have to find a new job and you might not be able to go to Disneyland anymore."

Does Age Matter?

Age Difference Between Kathie Lee and Frank Over Time

Year	Event	Kathie Lee's age	Frank Gifford's age
2003	Kathie Lee Gifford's 50th birthday	50	73
2007	Cody graduates from high school	54	77
2011	Cody graduates from college	58	81
2016	30th wedding anniversary	63	86
2018	Kathie Lee eligible to collect social security	65	88
2020	Cody's 30th birthday	67	90
2040	Cody's 50th birthday	87	110

Love Springs Eternal: Kathie Lee Gifford on Her Husband, Frank

"When he's away, I count the hours until he returns. I fully intend to be bubble-bathed with candles in it. Who knows what condition he'll be in? A girl can only hope."

What's wrong with this picture? Frank has been at a hotel where he has been wined and dined, while Kathie Lee has been home cleaning up Cody's playroom. Here's the way *we* picture the homecoming . . .

Frank: Kathie Lee, I'm home!
Kathie Lee: Your car is blocking mine. Move it.
Frank: Okay.
Kathie Lee: You're late. We already ate. Don't they have a telephone where you were?
Frank: Sorry, honey. What's for dinner?

Kathie Lee: What do I look like, Colonel Sanders? Did you pick anything up?

Frank: No, I—

Kathie Lee: Always thinking ahead!

Frank: I missed you, sweetheart.

Kathie Lee: I have gas. Give it a rest.

Frank: I love you, Kathie. I didn't mean to upset you. Perhaps we can have dinner out. A romantic dinner. Candlelight. Soft music. What do you say, honey?

Kathie Lee: I've got a headache.

10 Hors d'oeuvres You Can't Get at Kathie Lee's Dinner Parties

1. kasha varniskas

2. collard greens

3. burritos

4. potato latkes

5. hot pastrami

6. those little bits of raw fish rolled up in seaweed

7. Cheese Whiz fondue

8. beer nuts

9. Spam roll-ups

10. anything on a Ritz

Comments Most Frequently Uttered at Home by Frank Gifford While His Wife Is at Work:

"Help, I've fallen and I can't get up."

"Where's my upper plate?"

"I can't find the Playboy channel."

"24 . . . 48 . . . 24 . . . hike, hike, hike . . ."

"Where am I?"

Nine Best Things About Being Frank Gifford

1. Inexpensive to take family to movies—one adult, two children, one senior

2. Qualifies for special discount subscription to *Modern Maturity*

3. When doing his sportscast, is no longer expected to remember the names of the teams playing

4. Kathie Lee's fresh Miracle Whip® watercress sandwiches with the crusts cut off

5. Can now buy life insurance from Ed McMahon

6. At his age, *any* sex life is a great sex life

7. When he's 97, wife will still be a spring chicken

8. AARP pharmacy discount card

9. Looks pretty good when standing next to Wilford Brimley

Christmas at the Gifford House: Ten People You're Not Likely to See at Kathie Lee's Annual Tree Trimming Party

1. Ed Koch

2. Pee Wee Herman

3. Howard Stern

4. Deng Xiaopong

5. Margaret Thatcher

6. Stephen Hawking

7. Wayne Bobbitt

8. Courtney Love

9. Madonna

10. The skinny bug-eyed guy in the Little Caesar's Pizza commercials

Makes Ms. Manners Look Like Mother Theresa

"If he doesn't say 'please' he doesn't get something. If he doesn't say 'thank you' he doesn't get to keep what he's just been given. Other people thought that was a little too harsh at the beginning, and they say he doesn't even understand 'please' and 'thank you.' And I said all the more reason for him to learn to say it, so then it will be second nature. This is the way I was brought up."

—Kathie Lee Gifford on raising Cody

Surefire Ways to *Avoid* Seeing Kathie Lee on TV

1. Move to Albania

2. Develop cataracts

3. Watch the History Channel

4. Watch the Weather Channel

5. Go to the library

6. Work in a sweatshop where they don't have a TV set

7. Slip into a coma

6 Movie Scripts Kathie Lee Gifford is Currently Reading While Searching for Her Next Big Role

1. *Pope Fiction*

2. *Leaving Greenwich*

3. *Cody's Toy Story*

4. *The Bridges of Fairfield County*

5. *Perkiness and Sensibility: The Kathie Lee Gifford Story*

6. *Terminator IV: The Musical*

45 Entertainers and Celebrities Who Sing Better than Kathie Lee Gifford

Frank Sinatra

Frank Fields

Bruce Springsteen

Bruce Willis

Sandra Dee

Sander van Oker

Walter Cronkite

Sally Fields

Mrs. Fields

Kelsey Grammer

Kirstie Alley

Ted Danson

Connie Chung

Connie Francis

Francis Ford Coppola

Rosemary Clooney
George Clooney
Gerry Cooney
Joe Frazier
Pavarotti
Popeye
Leeza Gibbons
Roseanne
Nancy Sinatra
Barbara Sinatra
Cloris Leachman
Enrico Caruso
Ernest Borgnine
Jerry Vale
Gerry Ford
Swoozie Kurtz
Kurt Russell
Cyndi Lauper
Cindy Crawford
Amy Grant
Amy Carter

Fran Drescher

Fran Tarkenton

Barry Manilow

Bill Murray

Susan St. James

Rod McKuen

Roddy MacDowell

Phil Collins

Colin Powell

Kathy Lee, Inc.

Kathie Lee Gifford has numerous careers and businesses—all successful. In addition to being co-host of *Live* and hosting her annual Christmas special, her enterprises include: a line of clothing, record albums, books, children's videos, a television production company, an exercise video, and a soon-to-come skin care line.

In the spirit of supporting entrepreneurship and helping the Kathie Lee conglomerate grow even greater, here are some additional ideas for businesses and products she might want to consider:

Frank Gifford action figure doll

Line of autographed picture lunch boxes from Cody and Cassidy

Sexual instruction videotape filmed with her and Frank—*Sweating with the Oldie*

Jehovah's Witness Protection Program

A line of "grunge" clothes for Christians—"Holier Than Thou"

Little Caesar's pheasant under glass take-out

"Kathie Lee Gifford World" theme park

Top 10 Reasons Kathie Lee is Thinking About Leaving *Live With Regis and Kathie Lee*

1. Spend more time with Cody

2. Promote new line of power tools

3. Join the Peace Corps

4. Tour with Bette Midler

5. Design a Kathie Lee Gifford seder plate for Lalique

6. Wants to "spoil herself for a change"

7. More time to take down Christmas ornaments

8. Wants to reunite The Grateful Dead

9. Regis is an idiot

10. Gelman is a putz

Six Songs Kathie Lee is NOT likely to record

1. "These Boots Are Made for Walkin' "

2. "(I Don't Get No) Satisfaction"

3. "Younger than Springtime"

4. "September Song"

5. "Look For the Union Label"

6. "My Heart Belongs to Daddy"

Six Musicians Who Have Had a Profound Influence on Kathie Lee's Musical Career . . .

1. Alvin and the Chipmunks

2. Jim Nabors

3. The Mormon Tabernacle Choir

4. Kate Smith

5. Ferrante and Teischer

6. Marvin Hamlisch

. . . And Six Musicians Who Have Had NO Influence on Kathie Lee's Musical Career

1. Blood, Sweat, and Tears

2. Smashing Pumpkins

3. 10,000 Maniacs

4. Ray Charles

5. Placido Domingo

6. Vanilla Ice

Nine Jobs Kathie Lee Gifford Can Qualify For If She Leaves *Live with Regis and Kathie Lee*

1. Commander-in-Chief of the Salvation Army

2. Martha Stewart's stunt double

3. Press secretary for Princess Di

4. Sunday school teacher

5. Spokesperson for the Sugar Council

6. Substitute radio host for Rush Limbaugh

7. Newt Gingrich's personal assistant

8. Children's choir director

9. Mrs. Frank Gifford

From "The Day Ain't Over Yet" Department

"It was never my intention to 'market' my son as some have cynically claimed in the press. Anyone who thinks I was 'marketing' him should know about all the projects we have turned down because they were not the right sort of exposure for him."

—Kathie Lee Gifford, from her autobiography

From the "Wish We Had Said That" Department

"I . . . hate her (Kathie Lee Gifford). She's one of those pushy women who tell you how to live your life. They think they can sing, they think they can act, they never shut up about their husband or their kids or the Lord Jesus Christ."

> —TARA B., flight attendant and former member of the National Regis and Kathie Lee Fan Club, as quoted in *Allure*, June 1996

Merry Christmas!

"... A sickeningly saccharine vanity production that should really have been titled, O Come, Let us Adore Me."

—TOM SHALES, TV critic of

The Washington Post,

from his review of Kathie

Lee's Christmas special, 1996

10 Most Popular Baby Boy Names in the United States During the 8 Weeks Following Cody Gifford's Birth

1. Cody

2. Cody

3. Cody

4. Cody

5. Cody

6. Cody

7. Cody

8. Cody

9. Cody

10. Bob

Circle of Friends

"Kathie Lee's intelligence is off the charts. I mean, nobody I know is smarter."

—FRANK GIFFORD

Maybe he should get out more?

"I wish I was a little less ambitious."

—KATHIE LEE GIFFORD
ON KATHIE LEE GIFFORD

So do we, so do we!

"You ain't hip unless you watch Regis and Kathie Lee."

—ARSENIO HALL

And that's from someone who really knows *talk shows . . .*

What They Say about Kathie Lee Gifford, #87:

"My teeth rot just
watching her."
—Comedian NICK D'POLLO

The Truest Thing Kathie Lee Gifford Has Ever Said About Herself:

"Half the country wants
to throw up every time
they see me."

Kathie Lee Stupid and Offensive Comment #14:

"People resent the money Frank and I make, but they don't want to work as hard as we did. They'd rather be jealous."

A Winter's Tale

Leonard Nimoy, Dave Thomas, and Kathie Lee Gifford are traveling together during a long winter's night. Tired, they stop at a farmhouse to ask for shelter.

"There are only two guest bedrooms," says the farmer to the three celebrities. "So one of you will have to sleep in the barn with the animals."

Leonard Nimoy says, "I'll do it." But five minutes later, he is knocking at the front door. "There is a pig in the barn, but I am Jewish, so I cannot sleep there—pigs are unclean in our religion."

Being a gentleman, Wendy's founder Dave Thomas says he'll give up his room and sleep in the barn. But five minutes later, he is knocking at the front door. "There is a chicken in the barn, and I can't get to sleep because I'm constantly thinking of new chicken recipes for my restaurants."

Kathie Lee takes a blanket and goes out to the barn. But five minutes later, the farmer hears knocking again. He opens the front door of the house.

Standing outside are the pig and the chicken . . .

From the "So Stupid It's Funny" Department:

Recently, <u>Melrose Place</u> star Heather Locklear appeared as a guest on <u>Live with Regis and Kathie Lee</u>.

When asked about her character, Locklear replied that on the show, she was recently married to a new husband, Peter Burns.

Pausing a second, Locklear added a comment about how

"Peter Burns" struck her as an odd choice of name for the character.

Kathie Lee Gifford laughed.

Regis's comment: "I don't get it."

Neither Gifford nor Locklear seemed willing to explain it to him on the air.

Do they make Cliff Notes for jokes?

Meanwhile, rumor has it that two new characters will be

introduced on <u>Melrose</u> next year: Dick Hertz and Willie Soar.

Maybe Regis can audition for one of these parts?

Stern Talk about Kathie Lee Gifford

"Kathie Lee . . . has this phony-baloney quality and Pollyana attitude . . . The only reason I tune in every so often is because I want to have sex with her."

—Howard Stern

Inquiring Minds Want to Know. . . .

Why does Jane Pauley hate Kathie Lee Gifford. A "source" recently told the *National Enquirer* (8/27/96) that *Dateline NBC* host Jane Pauley allegedly said:

"It makes me cringe to hear Kathie Lee, in that sickeningly sweet voice, go on and on about how cute Cody and Cassidy are. The only reason she talks about her kids so much is . . . just to promote her own career."

Solving the Labor Crisis . . .

David Hinckley, TV critic for the *Daily News,* says: "The Giffords could solve this whole sweat-shop problem by having all the passengers on her cruise ships sew a couple of Kathie Lee blouses as one of their activities."

Cheap Women . . .

H. Meyer, in Letters to the Editor, *New York Daily News* (May 10, 1996):

"Gee whiz. Marla Maples and Kathie Lee Gifford. Career women and role models of the '90s. Two good-for-nothing home-wreckers— one got caught pulling up her pants, while one got caught making them cheap."

From David Letterman's Top 10 List . . .

One of the top 10 ways President Clinton could lower his approval rating with the American public: Have his jogging shorts made at Kathie Lee Gifford's sweatshop.

Over the Edge?

"Kathie Lee gives that little 'edge' to morning TV. Will she burst into tears, fly into a rage or just give us the latest on Cody and Cassidy? Admit it, love her or loathe her, it's hard to look away. And that's entertainment."

—Liz Smith, *NY Post,* 7/2/96

"Lord Give Me Strength"

"I pray every morning before I go on the air: Lord, please help me today. Don't let me hurt anyone with my mouth."

—Kathie Lee, 1992 (as quoted in *Time,* June 17, 1996)

Would You Buy a Used Car from This Woman?

"It's gotten to the point where you can flick on the TV day or night and see her smiling face, trying to sell you something."

—Joanna Powell, *Redbook* (July, 1992)

The 31-Cents an Hour Dream . . .

F. Saia, in Letters to the Editor, *New York Daily News,* June 4, 1996:

"Do not let Kathie Lee Gifford fool you. She has now hired a publicist to make her look good. She did wrong, and we all know it, because she is a pure phony. Imagine the publicity she'll gain. . . . They will sell more blouses this way, and more people will work for slave wages."

Survey Says . . .

Results from the Kathie Lee Gifford poll published in the July 6, 1996 issue of *TV Guide:*

* 41% of viewers admire Kathie Lee Gifford
* 62% think she talks too much about her troubles
* 56% said *Live with Regis & Kathie Lee* would be better off without her

Test Your Kathie Lee I.Q.

Answer the following questions as best you can. Then score yourself using the rating system below.

1. Which of the following companies has Kathie Lee Gifford *not* endorsed? (a) Carnival Cruise Lines (b) Home Furnishings Council (c) Ultra Slim Fast (d) Revlon (e) Wonder Bread (f) Coca Cola

2. What is Frank's pet name for Kathie Lee? (a) Big Momma (b) My Prime Time Love Machine (c) Yentl (d) Golda (e) Don Meredith with great legs (f) The She-Thing

3. Who described Kathie Lee's career as a "national 10-ring circus"? (a) Howard Stern (b) Don Imus (c) Frank Gifford (d) Kathie Lee Gifford (e) Regis Philbin

4. Kathie Lee has publicly stated she wants her marriage to be: (a) healthy (b) sexy (c) joyful (d) lasting (e) a TV special

5. What is Kathie Lee's pet name for Frank?
(a) Iron Buns   (b) This Old Man   (c) The Gipper
(d) Giff   (e) Biff

6. How long does it take Kathie Lee to commute from her Connecticut home to New York to co-host *Live?*   (a) 15 minutes—but only on the days she car-pools with Letterman   (b) zero—she is instantly transported by an invisible angel   (c) 60 minutes

7. Which of the following shows has Kathie Lee *not* worked on?   (a) *Name That Tune*   (b) *Beavis and Butthead*   (c) *A.M. Los Angeles*   (d) *Good Morning, America*   (e) *The Morning Show*   (f) *Days of our Lives*   (g) *I Believe in Miracles*   (h) *Hee Haw*

8. What is the title of Kathie Lee's best-selling 1992 autobiography?   (a) *I Can't Believe I Said That!*   (b) *Stop Me Before I Write More!*   (c) *People Like Me Better than Regis—So What!?*   (d) *The Gospel According to Kathie Lee Gifford*   (e) *Kathie Lee Gifford's Annotated Guide to the Bible*

9. Kathie Lee says her high school peers regarded her as: (a) a lily-white Penelope   (b) Miss Prom

Queen   (c) a "Miss Priss"   (d) busty   (e) a greaser
(f) droll

10. What's the first thing Kathie Lee does in the morning upon waking? (a) brush teeth   (b) comb hair   (c) use mouthwash   (d) shower   (e) pray that divine providence will keep her from offending or hurting anyone with her loquacity   (f) drink two cups of coffee and a glass of orange juice

11. Which of the following acts has Kathie Lee performed with?   (a) 10,000 Maniacs   (b) The Trapp Family Singers   (c) The Osmond Family: The Next Generation   (d) Devo   (e) Oral Roberts World Action Singers

12. Which of the following qualities does Kathie Lee say she has in abundance?   (a) personality (b) an innate curiosity   (c) a heart for people (d) wit and wisdom   (e) traditional values   (f) a killer slap shot

13. Kathie Lee suffers from the following malady: (a) bunions   (b) lycanthropy   (c) Chronic Fatigue Syndrome   (d) halitosis   (e) sainthood

14. An article in *New York Woman* described Kathie Lee's personality as: (a) darkly psychotic . . . in a Hannibal Lecter sort of way (b) perkiness bordering on carbonation (c) egomaniacal (d) controlling (e) a real downer

15. What is Cody's nickname for Frank? (a) Fossil Frank (b) This Old Man (c) Grandpa (d) Dinosaur Dad (e) Ancient of Days

16. Cody's godfather is: (a) Don Meredith (b) John Madden (c) Nelson Mandela (d) Walter Cronkite (e) Elie Weisel

17. Kathie Lee believes husbands should be (a) younger than their wives (b) about the same age as their wives (c) older than their wives (d) fossilized

18. Frank and Kathie Lee Gifford named their son Cody because (a) it sounded cute (b) it sounded original (c) it sounded hip (d) he is a descendent of Buffalo Bill (e) his nursery was large enough to have its own zip code (f) it is the name of Cody Riesen, a pro football player Frank knows

19. Which of the following events are we unlikely to see in this century?   (a) a democratic government in Cuba   (b) reappearance of Halley's comet (c) Jimmy Hoffa shopping at a local 7-Eleven   (d) pigs learning to fly   (e) Kathie Lee paying more than minimum wage in her sweatshops

20. Kathie Lee Gifford grew up in   (a) Bowie, Maryland   (b) Charleston, South Carolina   (c) Beverly Hills, California   (d) Kuala Lumpur   (e) Paris, France   (f) Disneyland

21. Which of the following is *not* a source of income for Kathie Lee?   (a) Warner Brothers   (b) Slim Fast   (c) Carnival Cruise Lines   (d) Halmode Apparel   (e) Americans for Democratic Action

22. The Gifford's dogs are named   (a) Merlot and Mateus   (b) Dr. and Mrs. Pepper   (c) Regis and Dumber   (d) Chardonnay and Chablis   (e) Thelma and Louise

23. Which of the following acts has Kathie Lee *not* opened for?   (a) Bill Cosby   (b) Rich Little   (c) Bob Hope   (d) Carrot Top   (e) Shecky Green

24. Kathie Lee Gifford says her "best aspects" include: (a) her personality   (b) an innate curiosity (c) a heart for people   (d) wit and wisdom rooted in a traditional take on life   (e) killer abs

25. Kathie Lee suffers from (a) allergies (b) bunions   (c) an ego more inflated than the Goodyear Blimp

ANSWERS: 1-e. 2-d. 3-d. 4-a, b, c, d. 5-d, f. 6-c. 7-b. 8-a. 9-a, c. 10-e. 11-e. 12-a, b, c, d, e. 13-a. 14-b. 15-d.* 16. We have no idea. 17-a, b, c. 18-f. 19-a, b, c, d. 20-a. 21-e. 22-a. 23-d. 24-a, b, c, d. 25-a, b.

SCORING: 1 point for every correct answer

Rating Your Kathie Lee I.Q.:

SCORE:	RATING:
0–1	You know as much as any sane person should know about Kathie Lee Gifford
2–3	We give you the benefit of the doubt: You're a lucky guesser.
4– or higher	For God's sake, get help . . . before it's too late!

*We're just guessing.

Eight Things We Actually *Like* About Kathie Lee Gifford

1. She's not the Unabomber.

2. She flosses regularly.

3. She's thinner than Oprah.

4. She rarely forgets to put a quarter in the parking meter.

5. She has not, as yet, been implicated in the assassination of either of the Kennedys.

6. She remembers to put the toilet seat down and the cap back on the toothpaste.

7. She maintains good eye contact with her manicurist.

8. She's quite life-like.

"I consider myself the least controversial person I have ever known."

—KATHIE LEE GIFFORD, MAY 16, 1996

Bibliography

Books

Cooking with Regis & Kathie Lee by Regis Philbin & Kathie Lee Gifford with Barbara Albright. New York: Hyperion, 1993. Let us know if you can resist the temptation to make the front cover into a dart board. Barbara Albright was Kathie Lee's ghostwriter on this book.

Entertaining with Regis & Kathie Lee by Regis Philbin & Kathie Lee Gifford with Barbara Albright. New York: Hyperion, 1994. This won't keep Martha Stewart up at night. Barbara Albright was Kathie Lee's ghostwriter on this book.

I Can't Believe I Said That! by Kathie Lee Gifford with Jim Jerome. New York: Pocket Books, 1992. Not quite as accurate as our book, but read it for backup. Jim Jerome was Kathie Lee's ghostwriter on this book.

Listen to My Heart: Lessons in Love, Laughter, and Lunacy by Kathie Lee Gifford and Cody Gifford. New York: Hyperion, 1995. Anecdote about Gerald and Betty Ford visiting the Giffords in Colorado is perhaps the most pointless story ever to make it into print. We think Cody was Kathie Lee's ghostwriter on this book.

Project Management: How to Plan and Manage Successful Projects by Joan Knutson and Ira Bitz. New York: Amacom, 1991. Gives you a good idea of how Kathie Lee's brain circuits must be wired.

Magazine Articles

"Can Kathie Lee Really Slow Down," by Deborah Norville, *McCall's,* February 1994, pp. 124–127.

"Dangerous Liaison," by Elizabeth Sporkin and Sue Carswell, *People,* September 30, 1991, pp. 34–39.

"Frank Talk with Kathie Lee," by Jennet Conant, *Ladies' Home Journal,* September 1993, pp. 134, 185–186.

"How Does She Do It?" by Barbara Lippert, *New York,* July 22, 1996, pp. 34–39.

"Kathie Lee, For Real," by Jill Brooke Coiner, *McCall's,* December, 1991, pp. 72–73, 128–133.

"Kathie Lee and Frank Gifford Finally Make It a Threesome," by Jeannie Park and Maria Eftimiades, *People,* May 21, 1990, pp. 162–164.

"Kathie Lee Gets Mad," by Ileane Rudolph, *TV Guide,* December 16, 1995, pp. 16–21.

"Kathie Lee Gifford," by Lawrence Eisenberg, *Good Housekeeping,* August, 1991, pp. 48–52.

"Kathie Lee Gifford," *Current Biography,* November 1994, pp. 30–34.

"Kathie Lee Gifford: 'I Have to Keep Growing Up,' " by Lawrence Eisenberg, *Good Housekeeping,* May 1994, pp. 161–162, 222.

"Kathie Lee Gifford: Talk Show Host and Entertainer," by Sharon Rose, *Newsmakers,* 1992 Cumulation. pp. 222–225.

"Kathie Lee's Greatest Hits," by Joanne Kaufman, *Ladies' Home Journal,* October 1992, pp. 128, 198–200.

"Kathie Lee's Hectic, Harried, and Very Happy Holidays," by Mary Alice Kellogg, *TV Guide,* December 17, 1994, pp. 12–14.

"Kathie Lee's Story," by Elizabeth Gleick and Sue Carswell, *People,* November 2, 1992, pp. 122–128.

"Kathie Lee: The Men in My Life," by Kathie Lee Gifford and Jim Jerome, *Good Housekeeping,* November 1992, pp. 186–187, 275–279.

"Kathie Lee: We Can't Believe She Said That!" by Meredith Berkman, *Redbook,* December, 1995, pp. 81–83, 112–114.

"My Life with Kathie Lee," Frank Gifford, *Good Housekeeping,* October 1993, pp. 107, 170–172.

"Up with Kathie Lee," by Joanna Powell, *Redbook,* July 1992, pp. 79–81, 116.

"We Just Went Too Far," by Roger Rosenblatt, *Time,* June 17, 1996, p. 104.

"Why the Gossips Can't Think of a Bad Word to Say About Kathie Lee Gifford," by Brigid O'Shaughnessy, *Redbook,* April 1993.

Newspaper Articles

"A Dressing Down," *Record,* June 30, 1996, p. A-2.

"Cheap Women," Letter to the Editor by H. Meyer, *Daily News,* May 10, 1996.

"Drop That Glue Gun: It's a Mock Martha," by Sherri Winston, *Record,* April 7, 1996.

"Fumble, Then Recovery," Jim Dwyer, Virginia Breen, William K. Rashbaum, and Jere Hester, *Daily News,* May 24, 1996, pp. 3–5.

"Jane Pauley: Why I Hate Kathie Lee," by Suzanne Ely, Jim Nelson, and Tony Brenna, *National Enquirer,* August 27, 1996, pp. 28–29.

"Kathie Lee Biz Giffs Back Pay," by Virginia Breen, *Daily News,* July 12, 1996, p. 26.

"Kathie Lee's High School Class Struggle," by George Rush and Joanna Molloy, *Daily News,* May 13, 1996, p. 14.

"Kathie Lee Gifford Rails at Clothing Industry," *Record,* June 1, 1996, p. A-10.

"Kathie Lee Rips Labor Big in TV Tirade," by Josef Adallan, *New York Post,* May 2, 1996.

"Kathie Lee's Sew Mad," by Corky Siemaszko, _Daily News,_ May 2, 1996, p. 8.

"Kathie Lee Slapped with Lawsuit for Abusing Elephant," by Jim Nelson, _National Enquirer,_ July 9, 1996.

"Kathie Lee Turned My Brother Against Me!" (interview with Lola Winona Gifford), _Globe,_ October 1, 1996, pp. 6–7.

"Live With Kathie Lee and Apparel Workers," by Steven Greenhouse, _The New York Times,_ May 31, 1996, p. B-3.

"Liz Smith" (column), _New York Post,_ July 2, 1996.

"Presenting Kathie Lee/Disney," by David Hinckley, _Daily News,_ June 25, 1996, p. 33.

"Teeing Off on Charity's Sunday Pitch," by David Hinckley, _Daily News,_ May 27, 1996, p. 33.

"The 31-Cents an Hour Dream," Letter to the Editor by F. Saia, _Daily News,_ June 4, 1996, p. 28.

About the Authors

GARY BLAKE is the author of *The Status Book* (Doubleday), a humorous look at status symbols. The book anticipated the status-conscious 1980s. Blake's humor and reviews have appeared in *College Board Review, Travel & Leisure, The New York Times Book Review, National Lampoon,* and many other periodicals.

BOB BLY is the author of more than 30 books including *The Ultimate Unauthorized Star Trek Quiz Book* (HarperCollins) and *What's Your Frasier I.Q.?* (Carol Publishing). His articles have appeared in *Cosmopolitan, City Paper, Amtrak Express, Writer's Digest,* and *New Jersey Monthly.*

Blake and Bly have co-authored eight books together including *Creative Careers: Real Jobs in Glamour Fields* (John Wiley & Sons). Their most recent collaboration is *The Elements of Business Writing* (Macmillan). They have been featured on dozens of radio and TV shows.

The authors point out that if Kathie Lee Gifford is offended by any of the contents of this book, it would be pointless for her to sue them, since she made more money last week than their total combined earnings during the entire 1990s (and the last quarter of 1989).

Questions and comments on *The "I Hate Kathie Lee Gifford" Book* may be sent to:

> Bob Bly and Gary Blake
> The Center for Technical Communicaton
> 22 E. Quackenbush Avenue
> Dumont, NJ 07628
>
> E-mail: Rwbly@aol.com